Old Snow

Also by Bei Dao

POETRY

The August Sleepwalker (1990)
translated by Bonnie S. McDougall

SHORT STORIES

Waves (1990)
translated by Bonnie S. McDougall
and Susette Ternent Cooke

Old Snow

TRANSLATED BY
BONNIE S. MCDOUGALL
AND CHEN MAIPING

A NEW DIRECTIONS BOOK

Acknowledgements

Some of these poems have previously appeared, occasionally in different ver-
sions, as follows. *Grand Street*: 'More unfamiliar than an accident . . .' and 'I
cannot see . . .'. *Manhattan Review*: 'The Morning's Story,' 'For Only a Sec-
ond,' 'The Collection,' 'The East's Imagination,' 'A Bach Concert,' 'Notes on
Reading,' 'Gains,' 'Coming Home at Night,' 'April' and 'Discovery.' *New
Directions 54*: 'The Bell,' 'An Evening Scene,' 'Restructuring the Galaxy,'
'Frostfall,' 'Requiem' and 'Along the Way'.

Manufactured in the United States of America
New Directions books are printed on acid-free paper
First published in the United States clothbound
and as New Directions Paperbook 727 in 1991
Published simultaneously in Canada by Penguin Books Canada Limited

Library of Congress Cataloging-in-Publication Data

Pei-tao, 1949–
    Old Snow : poems / Bei Dao ; translated by Bonnie S. McDougall and
Chen Maiping.
        p.   cm.
    Chinese and English.
    ISBN 0-8112-1182-7 (alk. paper). – ISBN 0-8112-1183-5 (pbk. :
alk. paper)
    1. Pei-tao, 1949–   –Translations into English.   I. McDougall,
Bonnie S., 1941–   .   II. Title.
PL2892.E525A25   1991
895.1'152–dc20   91-16507
                                                                        CIP

New Directions Books are published for James Laughlin
by New Directions Publishing Corporation
80 Eighth Avenue, New York 10011

旧雪

目　录

CONTENTS

PART III: STOCKHOLM

PREFACE

Most of the poems in Bei Dao's new collection *Old Snow* were written while the author was abroad. After obtaining a passport in 1985, he was finally able to accept the many invitations he had received to take part in poetry readings in Europe and America over the next few years, often accompanied by his wife, the painter Shao Fei, and their daughter, Tiantian. After a year in Durham, England, followed by a tour of the United States, he returned to China in late 1988 and again became actively involved in the movement for democracy and human rights. In the spring of 1989 he went to Berlin for a six-month visit, which was to be followed by three months in Oslo where he would once more be joined by his wife and child. He was in Berlin when the massacre of June 4 took place, and has remained abroad, alone, since that time. The poems in this collection reflect his initial forebodings, his overwhelming grief at the time of the massacre, and his anguish as the separation from his family was prolonged.

The eight poems in Part I were written between late 1988 and early June 1989. During the 1980s, Bei Dao found himself unable to join in the general optimism about the 'emancipation of the mind' and 'opening to the West' proclaimed by the Chinese authorities and welcomed by their friends abroad; he was too acutely aware of the continuing repressiveness of the régime's campaigns against 'spiritual pollution' and 'bourgeois liberalization'. Even as he took part in organizing the famous February 1989 letter of protest against the imprisonment of the democratic activist Wei Jingsheng, he expressed, in poems like 'The Bell', his fears that the movement would meet with bloody suppression. In 'Requiem', however, written a few days after June 4, there is a sense of faith and hope: it was hard for anyone in those days not to believe that this brutal use of terror must soon bring about the downfall of its perpetrators.

In September Bei Dao moved to Oslo, where he joined his old friend and collaborator Chen Maiping who had been living there since 1986. Together they set about reviving *Today*, their dissident literary magazine from the late 1970s, to provide a forum for Chinese writers like themselves suddenly in exile. A common theme in the poems from Part II is the experience of exile, cut off from home and family without warning, unable to return without possibly causing even more anguish to those nearest to him. During this time he was able to keep in touch by telephone, but the snows of Oslo's winter and the postman's Christmas holidays, described in 'Old Snow', intensified his feelings of isolation.

At the end of the year, Bei Dao moved to Stockholm, where he remained for another six months. It was clear by this time that he was facing an indefinite stay abroad with very little chance of being reunited with his family, and there is in the poems in Part III an attempt to cope philosophically with this realization. Returning to Oslo for the first meeting of a newly assembled editorial board of *Today* in May 1990, Bei Dao was also preparing himself for a post-Tiananmen vision of Chinese literature, where poetry whether written in exile or at home provides a means for the exploration of China's traditional and modern culture.

Readers of Bei Dao's earlier collection *The August Sleepwalker* have followed his course from early sentimentality, youthful defiance of arbitrary authority, tributes to love and friendship, and a steadily deepening pessimism. This collection still locates the author moving back and forth between public acts and private needs, but the reader is no longer offered the consolation of dreams, seclusion or shelter. The composition of the poems is still built around a sequence of powerful images, but the images are now more carefully chosen and thoughtfully structured.

Bei Dao's poems, although dubbed 'obscure' by orthodox Chinese literary critics, have never needed much in the way of annotation, and the only notes in this volume are to aspects of Chinese life which would need no explanation to the poet's first audience. References to Western place-names and events have become more common but are still general enough not to deter

Chinese readers. Occasionally the purely idiosyncratic or personal makes an appearance. At a dinner during one of his many visits to Europe in the late 1980s, his host informed him that the salt and pepper shakers on the table were called the Emperor and Empress; Bei Dao seems in 'Black Box' to have taken a family joke as a Western custom. Otherwise, Western readers are here invited to join their Chinese counterparts in reconstructing their own meanings in these sombre and compelling poems.

Peter Jay has again been the most generous and helpful of editors, and my co-translator and I are most grateful for his invaluable advice. We also wish to thank Peggy Fox for her untiring support and encouragement in both the British and American editions of this book.

B. McD.
June 1991

I
Berlin

钟声

钟声深入秋天的腹地
裙子纷纷落在树上
取悦着天空

我看见苹果腐烂的过程

带暴力倾向的孩子们
象黑烟一样升起
房瓦潮湿

十里风暴有了不倦的主人

沉默的敲钟人
展开的时间的幕布
碎裂,漫天飘零

一个个日子撞击不停

船只登陆
在大雪上滑行
一只绵羊注视着远方

它空洞的目光有如和平

万物正重新命名
尘世的耳朵
保持着危险的平衡

这是死亡的钟声

THE BELL

The bell tolls deep into autumn's hinterland
skirts scatter and fall on the trees
attempting to please the heavens

I watch the process of apples spoiling

children with a tendency to violence
ascend like black smoke
the roof tiles are damp

the three-mile storm* has tireless masters

time's curtain
opened by the silent bellringer
disintegrates, adrift in the sky

the days strike, one endlessly after the other

boats land
sliding on the heavy snow
a sheep stares into the distance

its hollow gaze resembles peace

all things are being renamed
the ears of this mortal world
maintain a dangerous balance

– It rings a death knell

---

* The students' parades along Peking's main street, Changan Avenue.

晚景

充了电的大海
船队满载着持灯的使者
逼近黑暗的细节

瞬间的刀锋
削掉一棵棵柏树上的火焰
枝干弯向更暗的一边

改变了夜的方向
山崖上的石屋
门窗开向四面八方

那些远道而来的灵魂
聚在光洁的瓷盘上
一只高脚蚊子站在中间

AN EVENING SCENE

On the electrified ocean
the fleet laden with messengers holding lamps
presses on towards the details of the dark

the moment's knife-edge
pares away the flames on each cypress
the branches curve towards the darker side

after having changed the night's direction
the stone house on the cliff
opens its doors and windows on all sides

the souls who've come from afar
collect on the bright clean china plate
a long-legged mosquito stands in the middle

重建星空

一只鸟 保持着
流线型的原始动力
在玻璃罩内
痛苦的是观赏者
在两扇开启着的门的
对立之中

风掀起夜的一角
老式台灯下
我想到重建星空的可能

无题

比事故更陌生
比废墟更完整

说出你的名字
它永远弃你而去

钟表内部
留下青春的水泥

RESTRUCTURING THE GALAXY

A bird preserves
its original streamlined mobility
inside the glass cover
it is the spectators who suffer
between two opposite
open doors

The wind lifts up a corner of the night
under the old-fashioned desk lamp
I consider the possibility of restructuring the galaxy

'MORE UNFAMILIAR THAN AN ACCIDENT . . . '

more unfamiliar than an accident
more complete than ruins

having uttered your name
it abandons you forever

youth's mud is left behind
inside the clock

霜降时节

大海改变以前
农民在死亡的一侧播种

奇蹄偶蹄人的足印
出入国家的大门

山也移动了一步
云杉点燃天上之火

运送矿砂的驳船
驶向皮毛高贵的夜晚

古老的欲望长鸣
故乡的灯火一起熄灭

FROSTFALL*

Before the ocean changes
the farmers sow the sector belonging to death

the footprints of perissodactyl and artiodactyl people
come and go through the nation's gates

even the mountain has shifted a step
the spruce tree lights heaven's fire

the barge conveying ore
steers towards the night in valuable furs

old desires blare
together the lights of home expire

---

* A two-week period in the traditional farmers' calendar, starting four
weeks after the autumn equinox.

悼亡
—— 为六 . 四受难者而作

不是生者是死者
在末日般殷红的天空下
结伴而行
苦难引导着苦难
恨的尽头是恨
泉水干涸, 大火连绵
回去的路更远

不是上帝是孩子
在钢盔与钢盔撞击的
声音中祈祷
母亲孕育了光明
黑暗孕育了母亲
石头滚动, 钟表倒转
日蚀已经出现

不是肉体是灵魂
每年一起再过一次生日
你们有同样的年龄
爱为死者缔造了
永久的联盟
你们紧紧拥抱
在长长的死亡名单中

REQUIEM

for the victims of June Fourth

Not the living but the dead
under the doomsday-purple sky
go in groups
suffering guides forward suffering
at the end of hatred is hatred
the spring has run dry, the conflagration stretches unbroken
the road back is even further away

Not gods but the children
amid the clashing of helmets
say their prayers
mothers breed light
darkness breeds mothers
the stone rolls, the clock runs backwards
the eclipse of the sun has already taken place

Not your bodies but your souls
shall share a common birthday every year
you are all the same age
love has founded for the dead
an everlasting alliance
you embrace each other closely
in the massive register of deaths

无题

我看不见
清澈的水池里的金鱼
隐秘的生活
我穿越镜子的努力
没有成功

一匹马在古老的房顶
突然被勒住缰绳
我转过街角
乡村大道上的尘土
遮蔽天空

'I CANNOT SEE ...'

I cannot see
the secret life
of the goldfish in the limpid pond
my efforts to pass through the mirror
have not succeeded

A horse on the ancient roof
is suddenly reined in
I turn the corner of the street
the dust on the village's main road
obscures the sky

在路上

七月，废弃的采石场
倾斜的风和五十只纸鹞掠过
向海跪下的人们
放弃了千年的战争

我调整时差
于是我穿过我的一生

欢呼自由
金沙的声音来自水中
腹中躁动的婴儿口含烟草
母亲的头被浓雾裹挟

我调整时差
于是我穿过我的一生

这座城市正在迁移
大大小小的旅馆排在铁轨上
游客们的草帽转动
有人向他们射击

我调整时差
于是我穿过我的一生

蜜蜂成群结队
追逐着流浪者飘移的花园
歌手与盲人
用双重光辉激荡夜空

我调整时差
于是我穿过我的一生

ALONG THE WAY

July, an abandoned stone quarry
the slanting wind and fifty paper hawks sweep by
the people kneeling towards the sea
have renounced their thousand year war

I adjust the time
so as to pass through my life

Hailing freedom
the sound of golden sands comes from water
the infant stirring in the belly has tobacco in its mouth
its mother's head is densely wrapped in fog

I adjust the time
so as to pass through my life

The city is migrating
hotels large and small are ranged on the tracks
the tourists' straw hats revolve
someone shoots at them

I adjust the time
so as to pass through my life

The bees in swarms
pursue the itinerants' drifting gardens
the singer and the blind man
agitate the night sky with their twofold glory

I adjust the time
so as to pass through my life

覆盖死亡的地图上
终点是一滴血
清醒的石头在我的脚下
被我遗忘

A drop of blood marks the final point
on the map spread over death
conscious stones underneath my feet
forgotten by me

II
Oslo

布拉格

一群乡下蛾子在攻打城市
街灯，幽灵的脸
细长的腿支撑着夜空

有了幽灵，有了历史
地图上未标明的地下矿脉
是布拉格粗大的神经

卡夫卡的童年穿过广场
梦在逃学，梦
是坐在云端的严厉的父亲

有了父亲，有了继承权
一只耗子在皇宫的走廊漫步
影子的侍从前簇后拥

从世纪大门出发的轻便马车
途中变成了坦克
真理在选择它的敌人

有了真理，有了遗忘
醉汉如雄蕊在风中摇晃
抖落了尘土的咒语

越过伏尔塔瓦河上时间的
桥，进入耀眼的白天
古老的雕像们充满敌意

有了敌意，有了荣耀
小贩神秘地摊开一块丝绒
请买珍珠聚集的好天气

PRAGUE

A swarm of country moths attack the city
street lamps, ghostly faces
slender legs supporting the night sky

Where there are ghosts, there's history
underground lodes unmarked on the map
are Prague's stout nerves

Kafka's childhood passed through the square
the dream plays truant, the dream
is the stern father, enthroned above the clouds

Where there's a father, there's a right of succession
a rat strolls through the palace corridors
shadowy attendants cluster round

The calèche that set out from the century's gate
has turned into a tank along the road
truth is choosing its enemies

Where there's truth, there's forgetfulness
swaying like a stamen in the breeze, the drunk
has dropped a dusty curse

Crossing time's bridge over the Vltava
one enters the dazzling daylight
the ancient statues are full of hate

Where there's hate, there's glory
the pedlar mysteriously spreads out a piece of velvet
please buy good weather where pearls join together

过节

毒蛇炫耀口中的钉子
大地有着毒蛇
吞吃鸟蛋的寂静
所有钟表
停止在无梦的时刻
丰收聚敛着
田野死后的笑容
从水银的镜子出发
影像成双的人们
乘家庭的轮子
去集市
一位本地英雄
在废弃的停车场上
唱歌

玻璃晴朗
桔子辉煌

CELEBRATING THE FESTIVAL*

The poisonous snake flaunts a nail in its mouth
on earth abides the silence
of snakes which swallow birds' eggs
all clocks and watches
stop at the dreamless moment
a bumper harvest gathers in
the smiling faces of dead fields
people with paired shadows
who set out from the mercury mirror
take the family wheels
to market
in an abandoned parking lot
a local hero
is singing

The glass shines bright
the orange gleams

* Refers to June 4, 1989. The students occupying Tiananmen Square
quoted Marx to the effect that revolution is the people's festival.

无题

他睁开第三只眼睛
那颗头上的星辰
来自东西方相向的暖流
构成了拱门
高速公路穿过落日
两座山峰骑垮了骆驼
骨架被压进深深的
煤层

他坐在水下狭小的舱房里
压舱石般镇定
周围的鱼群光芒四射
自由那黄金的棺盖
高悬在监狱上方
在巨石后面排队的人们
等待着进入帝王的
记忆

词的流亡开始了

'HE OPENS WIDE A THIRD EYE . . . '

He opens wide a third eye
the star above his head
warm currents from both east and west
have formed an archway
the expressway passes through the setting sun
two mountain peaks have ridden the camel to collapse
its skeleton has been pressed deep down
into a layer of coal

He sits in the narrow cabin under water
calm as ballast
schools of fish around him flash and gleam
freedom, that golden coffin lid
hangs high above the prison
the people queueing behind the giant rock
are waiting to enter the emperor's
memory

The exile of words has begun

早晨的故事

一个词消灭了另一个词
一本书下令
烧掉了另一本书
用语言的暴力建立的早晨
改变了早晨
人们的咳嗽声

蛆虫向果核进攻
果核来自迟钝的山谷
从迟钝的人群中
政府找到了它的发言人
猫与鼠
有相似的表情

空中之路
带枪的守林人查看
柏油的湖上
隆隆滚过的太阳
他听见灾难的声音
大火那纵情的声音

THE MORNING'S STORY

A word has abolished another word
a book has issued orders
to burn another book
a morning established by the violence of language
has changed the morning
of people's coughing

Maggots attack the kernel
the kernel comes from dull valleys
from among dull crowds
the government finds its spokesman
cats and mice
have similar expressions

On the road in the sky
the armed forester examines
the sun which rumbles past
over the asphalt lake
he hears the sound of disaster
the untrammelled sound of a great conflagration

知音

一只管风琴里的耗子
经历的风暴,停顿

白昼在延长
身体是大地的远景
绝对的辨音力
绝对的天空

一曲未终
作曲家的手稿飘散
被风暴收回

IN TUNE

The storm endured by the rat
inside the organ pauses

Daytime lengthens
the human figure is earth's far prospect
absolute true pitch
absolute sky

While the tune is yet unfinished
the composer's score blows away
recalled by the storm

旧雪

大雪复活了古老的语言
国家的版图变幻
在这块大陆上
一个异乡人的小屋
得到大雪的关怀

在我的门前
有一截三米长的钢轨

工厂倒闭，政府垮台
过期的报纸汇集着
变了质的大海
旧雪常来，新雪不来
造物的手艺失传
窗户后退
————五只喜鹊飞过

意外的阳光是一次事件

绿色的青蛙进入冬眠
这些邮差的罢工旷日持久
没有任何消息

OLD SNOW

When heavy snow revives an ancient language
maps of national territories change shape
on this continent
snow shows deep concern
for a foreigner's small room

Before my door
lies a three metre long steel rail

Factories go bankrupt, governments fall
outdated newspapers converge
into a decomposed ocean
old snow comes constantly, new snow comes not at all
the art of creation is lost
windows retreat
. . . five magpies fly past

Unexpected sunlight is an event

Green frogs start their hibernation
the postmen's strike drags on
no news of any kind

仅仅一瞬间

仅仅一瞬间
金色的琉璃瓦房檐
在黑暗中翘起
象船头闯进我的窗户
古老的文明
常使我的胃疼痛

仅仅一瞬间
青草酿造的牛奶沉寂
玻璃杯上
远处的灯光闪烁
这些环绕着死亡的
未来的嘴唇
有月亮的颜色

仅仅一瞬间
带着遗传秘密的男孩
奔跑中转过身来
从黎明的方向
用玻璃手枪朝我射击
弹道五光十色

仅仅一瞬间
气候习惯了我的呼吸
小雪,风力二级
松鸡在白色恐怖中飞奔
蚯蚓们在地下交谈
冬天里的情人
有着简单的语言

FOR ONLY A SECOND

For only a second
glazed golden eaves
rearing in the darkness
dash into my window like a prow
ancient civilization
makes my guts ache

For only a second
grass-fermented cow's milk falls silent
distant lights glitter
on the glass tumbler
the future's lips
encircling death
have the colour of the moon

For only a second
a boy holding heredity's secrets
turns in mid-run
from dawn's direction
and with a glass pistol shoots at me
polychromatic trajectories

For only a second
the climate is accustomed to my breath
light snow, wind force two
grouse take flight in the white terror
earthworms converse underground
lovers in winter
have a simple language

仅仅一瞬间
一把北京的钥匙
打开了北欧之夜的门
两根香蕉一只橙子
恢复了颜色

For only a second
a Peking key
opens the door of a Scandinavian night
two bananas and an orange
have recovered their original colour

绝症

星星在一面虚无的镜子中失去贞洁
从石像的嘴巴里传来可怕的预言

新世纪的舌头被四把铁锤轮流敲打
一个普通的词引起了森林大火

两只老虎在敌对的边境上做爱
太阳问世，摇荡着撒到舞台上的大海

恶劣的气候围困没有时间的窗户
权力在一块残旧的红布上过冬

一位历史的崇拜者因冲动而昏迷
做梦的空床用九十九只弹簧开始说话

TERMINAL ILLNESS

The stars have lost their chastity on a non-existent mirror
from the lips of a stone statue comes a terrible prophecy

The new century's tongue is beaten by four hammers in turn
an ordinary word stirs up forest fires

Two tigers make love on a hostile border
the sun comes on, rocking the ocean which has moved onstage

A foul climate surrounds the timeless window
power passes winter on a tattered red cloth

A history worshipper falls into a stupor through over-excitement
the dreaming empty bed begins to speak with ninety-nine springs

收藏

窗户为天空装上镜框
天空是我的收藏

黑色橡胶的山脉
世纪的夜晚
为星星命名的人听见
号角呜咽
那金属艰难的呼吸
在大地的围栏里
一个金属的婴儿诞生
打开的人类之书上
农舍向田野大声咒骂
扇子生病
追问季节的风淹没在海中
推移着千百只灯笼
为亡灵们照路

窗户为我装上镜框
我是天空的收藏

THE COLLECTION

The window makes a frame for the sky
the sky's in my collection

A black rubber mountain range
the century's evening
people who name stars can hear
the bugle sobbing
the metal's difficult breathing
a metal infant is born
inside earth's fence
on the open book of mankind
a peasant's hut curses loudly to the fields
the fan falls ill
the wind which interrogates the seasons drowns in the sea
shifting the thousands of lanterns which
light the way for the souls of the dead

The window makes a frame for me
I'm in the sky's collection

东方的想象

风中的钢刀灵巧地转动
大坝上的牛羊失踪
树木朝冬天一起鞠躬
绿色租赁给军队
枝干被造成大船时
洪水来临

豪华的时代
在宴请它的客人
铜号，美酒
竹椅上东方的想象
是不落的太阳
悬挂在砖窑上空

工匠们造就的天堂
流星般塌落
情人们睡在回声
那世纪之交的桥洞里
戴天使面具的人们
从桥上走过

THE EAST'S IMAGINATION

The steel knife in the wind turns neatly
the sheep and cattle above the dam are missing
the trees bow down together facing winter
green is rented to the troops
when branches are made into boats
floods approach

The luxurious age
invites its guests to a banquet
brass trumpets and fine wine
on the bamboo chair the East's imagination
is the sun which will not set
hanging in the air above the kiln

The paradise created by craftsmen
collapses like a falling star
lovers sleep in the echo
in the space beneath the bridge where the centuries meet
people with angel masks
cross over the bridge

III
Stockholm

占领

夜繁殖的一群蜗牛
闪闪发亮，逼近
人类的郊区
悬崖之间的标语写着：
未来属于你们

失眠已久的礁石
和水流暗合
导游的声音空旷：
这是敌人呆过的地方

少年跛脚而来
又跛脚奔向把守隘口的
方形的月亮

THE OCCUPATION

A troop of night-bred snails
glisten and shine, closing in
on humanity's outer suburbs
the poster hanging from cliff to cliff proclaims:
The future belongs to you

Insomnia-stricken reefs
conspire with streams
the tour guide's voice is vast:
This is where the enemy encamped

A youth limps forward
and sprints with a limp towards
the square moon guarding the pass

磨刀

我借清晨的微光磨刀
发现刀背越来越薄
刀锋仍旧很钝
太阳一闪

大街上的人群
是巨大的橱窗里的树林
寂静轰鸣
我看见唱头正沿着
一棵树桩的年轮
滑向中心

WHETTING

When I whet a knife with dawn's faint light
I find the spine getting sharper
while the blade stays blunt
the sun flares

the crowds in the high street
are trees in huge shop windows
the silence roars
I see the stylus gliding
along the tree stump's rings
towards the centre

此刻

那伟大的进军
被一个精巧的齿轮
制止

从梦中领取火药的人
也领取伤口上的盐
和诸神的声音
余下的仅是永别
永别的雪
在夜空闪烁

AT THIS MOMENT

The great advance
is checked
by an ingenious gear

The man who gets gunpowder from dreams
also gets salt on his wounds
and gods' voices
the remainder is only farewell
farewell snow
gleams in the night sky

纪念日

于是我们迷上了深渊

一个纪念日
痛饮往昔的风暴
和我们一起下沉

风在钥匙孔里成了形
那是死者的记忆
夜的知识

乡音

我对着镜子说中文
一个公园有自己的冬天
我放上音乐
冬天没有苍蝇
我悠闲地煮着咖啡
苍蝇不懂什么是祖国
我加了点儿糖
祖国是一种乡音
我在电话线的另一端
听见了我的恐惧

ANNIVERSARY

And now we're bewitched by a chasm

On one anniversary
the storm which consumes the past
sinks with us

Wind has taken shape in the keyhole
it is a remembrance of the dead
knowledge of night

A LOCAL ACCENT

I speak Chinese to the mirror
a park has its own winter
I put on music
winter is free of flies
I make coffee unhurriedly
flies don't understand what's meant by a native land
I add a little sugar
a native land is a kind of local accent
I hear my fright
on the other end of a phone line

黑盒

是谁在等待
一次预约的日出

我关上门
诗的内部一片昏暗

在桌子中央
胡椒皇帝愤怒

一支乐曲记住我
并卸下了它的负担

钟表零件散落
在王室的地平线上

事件与事件相连
穿过隧道

BLACK BOX

Who is it that waits
for a pre-appointed sunrise

I close the door
inside history it is dark

In the centre of the table
the Pepper Emperor is angry:

One dance tune remembers me
and lays down its burden

Clock parts scatter and fall
on the royal family's horizon

Events in a chain of succession
pass through the tunnel

巴赫音乐会

一颗罂粟籽挣脱了
鸟儿拨动风向的舌头
千匹红布从天垂落
人们迷失在
鲜艳的死亡中
巢穴空空
这是泄露天机的时刻

大教堂从波涛中升起
海下的山峰
带来史前的寂寞
左手变成玻璃
右手变成铁
我笨拙地鼓着掌
象一只登陆的企鹅

A BACH CONCERT

An opium-poppy seed struggles free from
the bird's tongue which bends the wind's direction
a thousand strips of red cloth hang from the sky
people lose their way in
brightly-coloured death
the bird's nest is empty
it is time to reveal the secret

A great cathedral rises from the waves
the mountains under the sea
bring a prehistoric solitude
my left hand turns into glass
my right hand turns into iron
I clumsily clap my hands
like a penguin on dry land

读书笔记

禁忌的花草
是历史的粮食

蝶钿的天空下
纸蝴蝶梦见
一个石头的家族

那颗胸中的红色棋子
驱使我向前
我是王或者卒
的影子,我遮蔽

隔岸的风雪
搅乱了另一个朝代的
激情

第五十代的耗子们
挥舞着长鞭

NOTES ON READING

Forbidden flowers and herbs
are history's foodstuffs

under a mother-of-pearl sky
the paper butterfly sees in a dream
a family of stones

the red chess-piece in my heart
drives me forward
I'm the king's or the pawn's
shadow, I hide from view

the snowstorm on the other bank
which has disrupted another dynasty's
fervour

fiftieth-generation rats
wave long whips

画
----给田田五岁生日

穿无袖连衣裙的早晨到来
大地四处滚动着苹果
我的女儿在画画
五岁的天空是多么辽阔
你的名字是两扇窗户
一扇开向没有指针的太阳
一扇开向你的父亲
他变成了逃亡的刺猬
带上几个费解的字
一只最红的苹果
离开了你的画
五岁的天空是多么辽阔

A PICTURE*

for Tiantian's fifth birthday

Morning arrives in a sleeveless dress
apples tumble all over the earth
my daughter is drawing a picture
how vast is a five-year-old sky
your name has two windows
one opens towards a sun with no clock-hands
the other opens towards your father
who has become a hedgehog in exile
taking with him a few unintelligible characters
and a bright red apple
he has left your painting
how vast is a five-year-old sky

* Tiantian, the nickname given to the poet's daughter, is written with
two characters which look like a pair of windows. The same character
also forms a part of the character for the word 'picture'.

展览会

沿着田野的一侧
推土机并列成长阵
我的白色夹克
在铲形的天空飞翔
而我被车灯照亮的头颅
穿过梦中的画廊
五十张地图
完全一样

THE EXHIBITION

Along one side of the field
a row of bulldozers forms a long front
my white jacket
soars in the scoop-shaped sky
while my skull illuminated by headlights
passes through the gallery in my dream
the fifty maps
are exactly the same

收获

一只蚊子
放大了夜的尺寸
它带着一滴
我的血

我是被夜的尺寸
缩小了的蚊子
我带着一滴
夜的血

我是没有尺寸的
飞翔的夜
我带着一滴
天堂的血

GAINS

A single mosquito
has enlarged night's size
taking a drop
of my blood

I am a mosquito
reduced by night's size
taking a drop
of night's blood

I am a sizeless
hovering night
taking a drop
of heaven's blood

双面镜

从镜中我们看见了
久远的事情:
碑林, 书桌焚烧后的
残存的腿
空中未干的墨迹

喧嚣来自镜子另一面

向上的未来之路
是巨型滑梯
从圣者的位置上
经历狂喜
我们从镜子里生下来

并永远留在这里
观望那久远的事情

THE DOUBLE-SIDED MIRROR

We've seen in the mirror
things from the distant past:
a forest of steles, the surviving legs
of desks that were set on fire
and undried ink marks in the sky

The noise comes from the other side of the mirror

The upward path of the future
is a gigantic slippery slide
after knowing delirious joy
from the sage's position
we are born from the mirror

And stay here forever watching
the things from a distant past

夜归

经历了空袭警报的音乐
我把影子挂在衣架上
摘下那只用于
逃命的狗的眼睛
卸掉假牙,这最后的词语
合上老 谋深算的怀表
那颗设防的心

一个个小时掉进水里
象深水炸弹在我的梦中
爆炸

COMING HOME AT NIGHT

After braving the music of the air raid alarm
I hang my shadow on the hat-stand
take off the dog's eyes
(which I use for escape)
remove my false teeth (these final words)
and close my astute and experienced pocket watch
(that garrisoned heart)

The hours fall in the water one after the other
in my dreams like depth bombs
they explode

信

你在哪儿
玫瑰的海岬在哪儿
穿过火焰的路在哪儿
不记誓言的山峰在哪儿
身体象蚌壳般合上的
那颗珍珠在哪儿
末日前的狂欢节在哪儿
旗帜上的彗星在哪儿
大雾的中心在哪儿
你在哪儿
我们在哪儿

THE LETTER

where are you
where is the strait of roses
where is the path through the fire
where is the peak that forgets its oath
where is the pearl
whose body shuts like a clam
where is the pre-doomsday carnival
where is the flag's victorious star
where is the dense fog's centre
where are you
where are we

致记忆

你步步逼近
暗含杀机
而我接受惩罚
所有的审判
是一种告别仪式

我们将交换角色
通过音乐之虹

在另一世界
我是化石
你是流浪的风

TO MEMORY

You close in on me, step by step
with a secret intent to kill
while I accept punishment
all trials
are a farewell ceremony

We may change rôles
through the rainbow of music

In another world
I am a fossil
you are the roaming wind

祖国

黑伞下的少女
钟舌般摆动
我悄悄地潜入森林
听见声响时回头
那只鹿已消失

月光为粗糙的冬天
涂着清漆
在地板的缝隙下
海水激荡不安
我正在和我
修复了的你的尊严
告别

MY COUNTRY

The young woman under the black umbrella
sways like a pendulum
I slip quietly into the forest
hearing a noise I turn round
the deer has already vanished

Moonlight spreads a varnish
over the rough winter
under the cracks in the floorboards
sea water surges restlessly
and now I bid farewell
to what I've restored
– your dignity and honour

写作

始于河流而止于源泉

钻石雨
正在无情地剖开
这玻璃的世界

打开水闸，打开
刺在男人手臂上的
女人的嘴巴

打开那本书
词已磨损，废墟
有着帝国的完整

COMPOSITION

starts in the stream and stops at the source

diamond rain
is ruthlessly dissecting
the glass world

it opens the sluice, opens
a woman's lips
pricked on a man's arm

opens the book
the words have decomposed, the ruins
have imperial integrity

四月

四月的风格不变:
鲜花加冰霜加抒情的翅膀

海浪上泡沫的眼睛
看见一把剪刀
藏在那风暴的口袋中

我双脚冰凉, 在田野
那阳光鞣制的虎皮前止步

而头在夏天的闪电之间冥想
两只在冬天聋了的耳朵
向四周张望 ——

星星, 那些小小的拳头
集结着浩大的游行

APRIL

April's style doesn't alter:
flowers plus frost plus lyrical wings

Bubbling eyes on the ocean
see a pair of scissors
hidden in the storm's pocket

My feet freeze, halting in front of
the field (a tiger-skin tanned in the sun)

And my head ponders between flashes of summer lightning
my ears grown deaf during winter
gaze on all sides

Stars (these small fists)
combine to form a massive demonstration

叛逆者

那取悦于光的影子
引导我穿行在
饮过牛奶的白杨
和饮过血的狐狸之间
象条约穿行在
和平与阴谋之间

披外套的椅子坐在
东方，太阳是它的头
它打开一片云说：
这里是历史的终结
诸神退位，庙堂锁上
你仅仅是一个
失去声音的象形文字

REBEL

The shadow which tries to please the light
leads me to pass between
the aspen that has drunk milk
and the fox that has drunk blood
like a treaty passing between
peace and conspiracy

The chair draped with an overcoat sits
in the east, the sun is its head
it opens a cloud and says:
here is the end of history
the gods have abdicated, the temples are locked
you are nothing but
a pictograph that's lost its sound

发现

城市的仙人掌
这些多情的移民
分散，却以刺和花结盟
从溺水者的口中取冰
在黄金的文火上取暖
上帝，烟雾如龙
牵着狗的女人
是没有终点的末班车
醉汉们搭乘的是梦

我从风景和暴行中归来
穿过四季的转门
在下着雪的房间里
找到童年的玩具
和发条上隐秘的刻痕

DISCOVERY

City cactus
(these affectionate migrants)
scatter, but use thorns to form an alliance with flowers
taking ice from the mouth of the drowned
drawing heat from the gold's low flame
God is – smoke like a dragon
the woman leading a dog
is the last train, with no destination
what the drunks get on is a dream

I come back home from landscapes and atrocities
passing through the four seasons' revolving door
in the room where it is snowing
I find my childhood toys
and a secret mark on the clockwork springs